Lerner SPORTS

ALL-STAR SMACKDOWN

ALEX MORGAN VS. MIA HAMM

WHO WOULD WIN?

JOSH ANDERSON

Lerner Publications ◆ Minneapolis

Lerner Publications Company
An imprint of Lerner Publishing Group, Inc.
241 First Avenue North
Minneapolis, MN 55401 USA

For reading levels and more information, look up this title at www.lernerbooks.com.

Main body text set in Aptifer Sans LT Pro.
Typeface provided by Linotype AG.

Library of Congress Cataloging-in-Publication Data

Names: Anderson, Josh, author.
Title: Alex Morgan vs. Mia Hamm : who would win? / Josh Anderson.
Other titles: Alex Morgan verus Mia Hamm
Description: Minneapolis, MN : Lerner Publications, [2024] | Series: Lerner sports. All-star smackdown | Includes bibliographical references and index. | Audience: Ages 7–11 | Audience: Grades 4-6 | Summary: "Alex Morgan and Mia Hamm are two of the greatest scorers in US soccer history. Learn about their triumphs on and off the field, compare their stats, and then choose a winner"— Provided by publisher.
Identifiers: LCCN 2023013878 (print) | LCCN 2023013879 (ebook) | ISBN 9798765610282 (library binding) | ISBN 9798765623534 (paperback) | ISBN 9798765614020 (epub)
Subjects: LCSH: Hamm, Mia, 1972—-Juvenile literature. | Morgan, Alex (Alexandra Patricia), 1989—-Juvenile literature. | Women soccer players—United States—Biography—Juvenile literature. | BISAC: JUVENILE NONFICTION / Sports & Recreation / Soccer | JUVENILE NONFICTION / Biography & Autobiography / Sports & Recreation
Classification: LCC GV942.7.H27 A75 2024 (print) | LCC GV942.7.H27 (ebook) | DDC 796.334092 [B]—dc23/eng/202303234

LC record available at https://lccn.loc.gov/2023013878
LC ebook record available at https://lccn.loc.gov/2023013879

Manufactured in the United States of America
1 – CG – 12/15/23

TABLE OF CONTENTS

Mia Hamm

INTRODUCTION

LEGENDS OF THE GAME

In 1991, teams from around the world played in the first FIFA Women's World Cup. Mia Hamm was only 19 years old. She was the youngest player on the US Women's National Team (USWNT).

» FAST FACTS «

- Mia Hamm played for the US in four FIFA Women's World Cups.
- Hamm led the University of North Carolina to four championships during her college career.
- Alex Morgan played for the USWNT during two Olympic Games.
- During Morgan's one season playing for Lyon in France, the team won three major events.

In their first game, the US held a 2–0 advantage over Sweden in the 62nd minute of the 90-minute match. But the team wanted to score again. The US had come to the tournament with the goal of being the first Women's World Cup champions.

Hamm dribbled the ball. She dashed around her defender's right side. From just outside the penalty area, Hamm kicked the ball. It flew over the goalkeeper and into the net. Sweden scored two goals later in the game. But Hamm's goal was the game winner. The US won 3–2. Hamm scored many important goals for the US in her incredible career.

Twenty years later, Alex Morgan was the youngest player on the USWNT at the 2011 Women's World Cup. She wasn't a starter, but she played in every game. Morgan had not scored in the tournament.

The US and France were locked in a tight match. The US held a 2–1 lead. During the game's 82nd minute, Morgan and teammate Abby Wambach ran up the field with the ball. Four French defenders ran with them. Wambach passed the ball ahead, and everyone ran for it. But Morgan came away with the ball.

She dribbled toward the goal and took a shot just inside the penalty area. The ball barely touched the tips of the goalkeeper's fingers as it went into the net. Morgan's first goal of the World Cup helped seal the victory for the US. The USWNT lost the championship match to Japan. But Morgan would have many more glory days ahead.

Hamm and Morgan are two of the most successful pro soccer players of all time. But which one was the best? Let the smackdown begin!

Alex Morgan** (center) **scores against France in the 2011 FIFA Women's World Cup.

Alex Morgan (top) celebrates with teammate Lauren Holiday after Morgan scored a goal in the 2011 Women's World Cup.

CHAPTER 1

Mia Hamm (left) prepares to shoot in a 1989 game.

JOURNEY TO SUCCESS

Mia Hamm was born March 17, 1972, in Selma, Alabama. Her father was in the US Air Force. They lived on air force bases in many different parts of the world.

Mia first tried soccer when her family was living in Florence, Italy. She played on her first team at the age of five in Texas. Mia was a good athlete and enjoyed many sports as a kid. She even played on her junior high school's football team.

Mia was the best player on her high school soccer team. She

was such a strong player that she got the chance to play for the USWNT at just 15. Mia's first match was at the 1987 US Olympic Festival in North Carolina.

Hamm attended the University of North Carolina (UNC) at Chapel Hill. During her college career, Hamm led the North Carolina Tar Heels to four national championships. She won

Hamm (right) dribbles away from a defender at the 1987 US Olympic Festival.

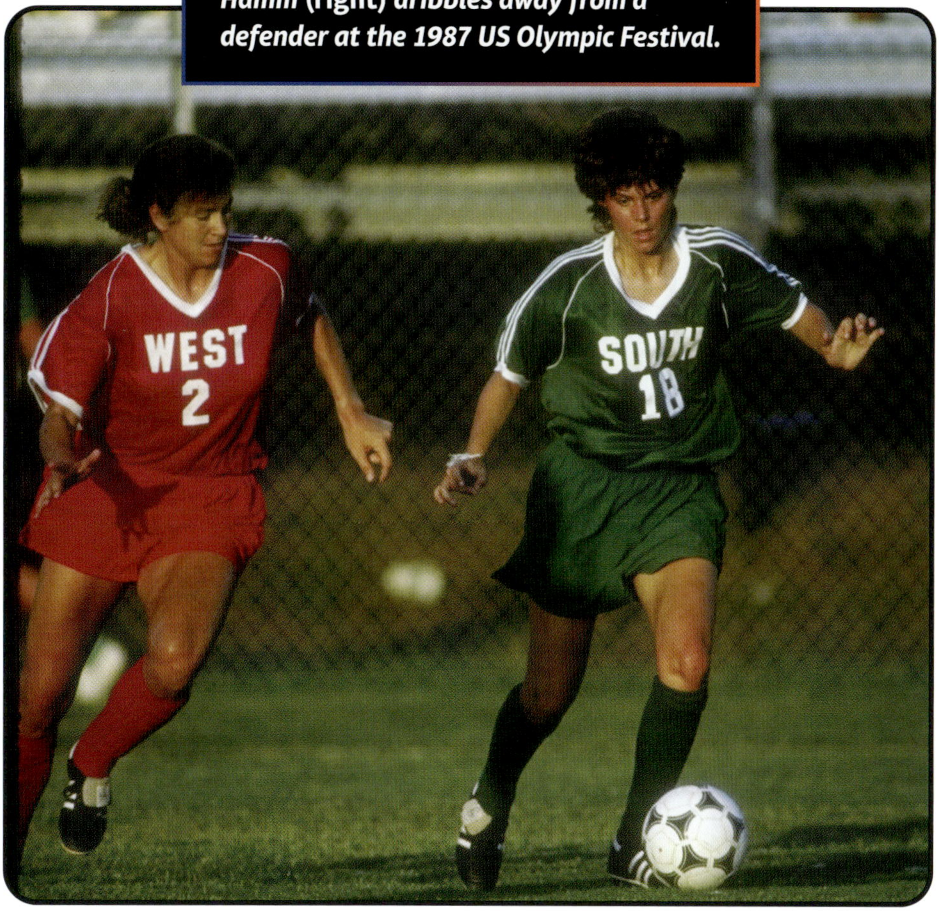

the Atlantic Coast Conference Player of the Year award three years in a row. Hamm played 95 games for UNC, and the team won 92 of them.

Alex Morgan was born July 2, 1989, in San Dimas, California. She played several sports and didn't focus on soccer until she was 14. When she did finally join a soccer team, she helped lead them to the league championship.

Hamm takes a shot during soccer practice at the University of North Carolina.

Morgan (left) battles Stanford's Allison Falk for the ball.

Morgan was an All-American during high school. She was also invited to play in the Olympic Development Program. This program provides high-level training to promising young soccer stars.

Morgan played four seasons for the University of California, Berkeley. She led the team to the national college tournament each year. As a freshman, she led the team in scoring. She ranks third all-time in goals scored at the school.

Morgan began her Team USA career playing for the Under-20 Women's National Team in 2008.

CONSIDER THIS

The United States has only had a women's national soccer team since 1985. When the team started, women's soccer was not yet part of the Olympic Games and the Women's World Cup did not exist.

In 2010, Morgan played her first game with the top level of the USWNT. They beat Mexico 1–0. She scored her first goal for the team in a 1–1 tie later that year against China.

Morgan (right) tries to take the ball during a game against Mexico in 2011.

CHAPTER 2

Hamm (left) tries to outrun Cecilia Sandell of Sweden during the 1996 Olympics.

GREAT MOMENTS

Hamm was the youngest player on the USWNT in 1991. But that did not stop her from being a key part of the team's offense. She started five of the team's six games in the first FIFA Women's World Cup and scored two goals. The US won the tournament without losing a single game.

The USWNT finished third at the 1995 FIFA Women's World Cup. But they had their sights set on gold at the 1996 Olympic Games in Atlanta, Georgia. It was the first Olympic Games to include women's soccer. Hamm fought through injuries to lead the US to a gold medal. In the final game, the team competed in front of more than 76,000 fans. It was the largest crowd ever for a women's sporting event in the US.

One of the most high-pressure moments in Hamm's career came in the final game of the 1999 FIFA Women's World Cup. Neither team scored in 90 minutes of regular play and 30 minutes of extra time. The match came down to penalty kicks. Each team would take five shots. The team that scored the most would win the trophy.

Hamm runs down the field in the 1999 Women's World Cup final.

Hamm** (center left) **celebrates with teammates after winning the 1999 Women's World Cup.

The score was tied 3–3 when Hamm stepped up to take the fourth shot for Team USA. She sent the ball flying into the right side of the net. After teammate Brandi Chastain scored the final penalty kick, the US celebrated its second Women's World Cup victory. With two goals and two assists, Hamm made the tournament's All-Star team. The win made women's soccer more popular in the US. Many girls decided to play soccer after cheering on the 1999 USWNT.

Shortly before she retired from Team USA, Hamm led the US to its second gold medal at the 2004 Olympics in Athens, Greece. The US Olympic team chose Hamm to carry the country's flag at the closing ceremonies. It was the perfect

CONSIDER THIS

In 2019, *Time* magazine picked Alex Morgan as one of its 100 most important people. Mia Hamm wrote the article that honored Morgan.

way to honor one of the greatest players in soccer history.

In 2011, Morgan helped lead the USWNT to the FIFA Women's World Cup final. She was the youngest player on the team. The US lost to Japan in penalty kicks, but Morgan became the first player with a goal and an assist in a Women's World Cup final.

Morgan controls the ball between two defenders at the 2011 Women's World Cup final against Japan.

One of Morgan's most memorable moments came late in a match against Canada at the 2012 Olympics in London, England. The score was tied 3–3. In the final seconds of extra time, US forward Abby Wambach passed to Heather O'Reilly. O'Reilly passed the ball near the goal.

Morgan ran forward, leaped into the air, and tapped the ball with her head. It flew over the arm of Canada's goalkeeper and into the net. Morgan's goal sent the US to the gold medal game against Japan. She had an assist in Team USA's 2–1 victory.

Morgan runs past a Team Canada defender on the ground during the 2012 Olympic Games.

The USWNT celebrates winning the 2019 FIFA Women's World Cup.

In 2019, Morgan scored six goals at the FIFA Women's World Cup. No other player scored more goals than Morgan did. She helped the US win its fourth Women's World Cup trophy.

One of Morgan's greatest wins happened off the field. She had spoken out for years about unfair pay. The US Men's National Team players earned more money than the USWNT players did. After a six-year battle with US Soccer, Morgan and her teammates finally won. They signed a contract that provided the women's team equal pay and prize money. Morgan and her teammates' victory for equal pay will have a long-lasting impact on women's soccer.

CHAPTER 3

Morgan points to the cheering crowd after scoring for the USWNT at the 2019 FIFA Women's World Cup.

SUPER STRIKERS

Hamm and Morgan are two of the most successful soccer players in the history of the sport. Hamm competed in four FIFA Women's World Cup tournaments. She helped lead the US to victory twice, in 1991 and 1999. Morgan has competed in three Women's World Cups for the US, earning two first place finishes. She is also a member of the team that will compete at the 2023 FIFA Women's World Cup.

Both Hamm and Morgan played for the USWNT in three

Olympics. Hamm won two gold medals and one silver. Morgan has won one gold medal and one bronze medal.

Morgan is tied for 10th in USWNT history with 49 assists. Hamm is the all-time leader in assists with 144. Hamm ranks second behind Abby Wambach on the all-time list of goals scored with 158. Morgan is fifth with 121. The top-scoring men's national team player, Cristiano Ronaldo of Portugal, has only scored 120 goals.

Hamm is in fifth place all-time with 276 games for the US Women's National Team. Morgan is farther down the list,

Hamm (right) celebrates with teammate Abby Wambach during a 2003 match.

CONSIDER THIS

Hamm and Morgan are the only two US women to score at least 20 goals and 20 assists for the USWNT in the same year. Hamm did it in 1998, while Morgan did it in 2012.

tied for 27th place with 206 appearances. In 2012, Morgan won the US Soccer Female Athlete of the Year award. Hamm was named US Soccer Female Athlete of the Year five times. She was the FIFA World Player of the Year twice, in 2001 and 2002.

Hamm takes a shot for the Washington Freedom in 2001.

Morgan* (front row, third from right) *and supporters celebrate winning their fight with US Soccer for equal pay.

Both Hamm and Morgan are great leaders in women's soccer. Hamm was a pioneer of the sport in the US. She played in the first FIFA Women's World Cup and the first Olympics to include women's soccer. Hamm is also a co-owner of Los Angeles FC, a Major League Soccer team, and Angel City FC of the National Women's Soccer League.

Morgan used her voice to fight for equal pay for the USWNT. She is one of the team's all-time greatest scorers. Morgan has been a superstar and a leader for her team on and off the field.

CHAPTER 4

Morgan celebrates during a match against the Netherlands at the 2020 Olympics.

AND THE WINNER IS

Who is the winner of this all-star soccer smackdown? You can decide for yourself. Hamm and Morgan are among the greatest soccer players of all time, so there is no right or wrong answer. Different people may have different opinions. That's part of the fun of being a sports fan. So who do you think is best?

Each player has been an important member of the USWNT at the FIFA Women's World Cup. Hamm and Morgan both won the big prize twice. Morgan has a chance to win a third Women's World Cup in 2023.

Hamm holds a big advantage in assists, 144 to 49. But Hamm's Team USA career spanned 17 years. Morgan's USWNT career began in 2010.

Hamm scored her 101st goal for Team USA in 1998. She went on to score 57 more before she retired in 2004.

Hamm scored 158 goals for the USWNT. Morgan scored 121 times from 2010 to 2022. She has averaged 11 goals per year, while Hamm averaged just over 9.

It's very hard to choose a winner in a contest this close. Morgan may one day overtake Hamm as a goal scorer, but Hamm is the winner of this smackdown. Hamm's amazing career made her the best and most exciting woman ever to set foot on a soccer field. Who do you think the winner is? Think it over and make your choice!

Morgan holds up her bronze medal at the 2020 Olympics in Tokyo, Japan.

Hamm leads her team during the 1999 FIFA Women's World Cup.

SMACKDOWN BREAKDOWN

MIA HAMM

Height: 5 feet 5 (1.7 m)
USWNT goals: 158
USWNT assists: 144
FIFA Women's World Cup championships: 2
Olympic gold medals: 2

Stats are accurate through April 2023.

ALEX MORGAN

Height: 5 feet 7 (1.7 m)
USWNT goals: 121
USWNT assists: 49
FIFA Women's World Cup championships: 2
Olympic gold medals: 1

GLOSSARY

All-American: a top player at the high school or college level in the US

assist: a pass that leads directly to a goal

club: a pro soccer team

dribble: to move and control the soccer ball with the feet

FIFA: a group that oversees soccer around the world

forward: a soccer player whose main job is scoring goals

hat trick: when a player scores three goals in a game

penalty area: an area in front of each goal on a soccer field within which a broken rule by a defending player might cause a penalty kick to be awarded to the opposing team

penalty kick: a free kick at the goal allowed for certain fouls or to decide the winner of some games

pioneer: a person who leads the way for others

starter: a player who is on the field at the beginning of a game

LEARN MORE

Alex Morgan Official Site
https://alexmorgansoccer.com/

Jökulsson, Illugi. *Alex Morgan*. New York: Abbeville Kids, 2020.

Levit, Joe. *Mia Hamm: Striking Gold*. Minneapolis: Lerner Publications, 2022.

Oxenham, Gwendolyn. *Pride of a Nation: A Celebration of the U.S. Women's National Soccer Team*. New York: Ten Speed Press, 2022.

Sports Illustrated Kids—Soccer
https://www.sikids.com/tag/soccer

U.S. Women's National Team
https://www.ussoccer.com/teams/uswnt

INDEX

PHOTO ACKNOWLEDGMENTS

Image credits: David Madison/Contributor/Getty Images, p.4; Franck Seguin/Contributor/Getty Images, p.5; PATRIK STOLLARZ/Staff/Getty Images, p.6; Scott Heavey/Staff/Getty Images, p.7; The Washington Post/Contributor/Getty Images, p.8; Getty Images/Staff/Getty Images, p.9; Will & Deni McIntyre/Contributor/Getty Images, p.10; San Francisco Chronicle/Hearst Newspapers via Getty Images/Contributor/Getty Images, p.11; Alex Livesey - FIFA/Contributor/Getty Images, p.12; Nick Laham/Staff/Getty Images, p.13; Stephen Dunn/Staff/Getty Images, p.14; David Madison/Contributor/Getty Images, p.15; Jed Jacobsohn/Staff/Getty Images, p.16; Friedemann Vogel/Stringer/Getty Images, p.17; Jamie McDonald - FIFA/Contributor/Getty Images, p.18; Naomi Baker - FIFA/Contributor/Getty Images, p.19; Richard Heathcote/Staff/Getty Images, p.20; Al Messerschmidt/Staff/Getty Images, p.21; Greg Fiume/Stringer/Getty Images, p.22; Ira L. Black - Corbis/Contributor/Getty Images, 23; Laurence Griffiths/Staff/Getty Images, p.24; Ezra Shaw/Staff/Getty Images, p.25; Alex Grimm - FIFA/Contributor/Getty Images, p.26; David Madison/Contributor/Getty Images, p.27; Al Messerschmidt/Staff/Getty Images, p.28; Tottenham Hotspur FC/Contributor/Getty Images, p.29

Cover: Elsa/Staff/Getty Images; Megan Briggs/Contributor/Getty Images